MAKE MONEY NOW!™

MONEY-MAKING OPPORTUNITIES FOR TEENS
WHO LIKE WORKING OUTSIDE

TAMRA B. ORR

ROSEN PUBLISHING®

New York

Published in 2014 by The Rosen Publishing Group, Inc.
29 East 21st Street, New York, NY 10010

Library of Congress Cataloging-in-Publication Data

Orr, Tamra B.
Money-making opportunities for teens who like working outside/
Tamra B. Orr.—1st ed.
    p. cm.—(Make money now!)
Includes bibliographical references and index.
ISBN 978-1-4488-9383-6 (library binding)
1. Vocational guidance—Juvenile literature. 2. Teenagers—Employment—
Juvenile literature. 3. Job hunting—Juvenile literature. I. Title.
HF5381.2.O77 2014
650.10835—dc23

                                                                    2012040029

Manufactured in the United States of America

CPSIA Compliance Information: Batch #S13YA: For further information, contact Rosen Publishing, New York, New York, at
1-800-237-9932.

CONTENTS

Hungry Portlanders have a lot of choices when it comes to eating. Besides the usual chain and independently owned restaurants, a growing number of the Oregon city's once empty parking lots are now filling up with a variety of carts, or mobile kitchens, and creating what is called a "Cartopia." In one corner, a shiny silver cart features a fascinating mix of Swedish and African American foods known as "Viking soul food." Over here you can taste a London pasty, a gourmet European version of a beef patty. Like hot dogs? Try this stand—it has a dozen different flavors of dogs and even more toppings. Does your sweet tooth crave a little dessert? You might try the ice cream stand where they feature local flavors such as lavender lemon or maple bacon. Of course, if you just want a burger and fries, you can find those, too, but don't be surprised if the burger is topped with peanut sauce and cucumbers, and the fries are covered with generous sprinkles of sea salt and parmesan cheese.

As popular as these carts have become, a few determined vendors have taken convenient and delicious food a

Erika Kraner and Melanie McClure, the owners and operators of the street food vendor Taco Pedaler, prepare and serve their delicious food on the streets of Portland, Oregon.

step further. Instead of providing a dozen carts in a circle for people to visit, these business owners are literally bringing the food to the people. When they say they are mobile, they really mean it. One such vendor is the Taco Pedaler, a small business created in 2010 and run by friends Erika Kraner and Melanie McClure. Each day, they put on their sturdy sneakers, stretch their muscles, and climb on their bikes. It's time to bring home-made Mexican treats to the people of downtown Portland!

A few years ago, Kraner and McClure were vacationing in Mexico. Their favorite place to eat was found right on the beach. It was a bicycle that had a grill built in, known in Mexico as a *triciclo de carga*. Each day, tourists lined up to eat burritos and tacos made right there in front of them, with the freshest of ingredients. The two young women were inspired. They knew that Portland was one of the most bicycle friendly communities in the country. Kraner and McClure had always loved riding their bikes and being outside—so could they turn that into a business?

Today, it is clear that the answer to that question is yes. Taco Pedalers is a familiar business in downtown Portland. It recently won an award for the cart with the "most style." Kraner and McClure are expanding from just a couple of bikes to several and hoping to open an actual storefront in the coming months.

It's not an easy job. The bicycles, which were imported from Mexico, weigh hundreds of pounds each. Kraner custom designed them to include grills, cutting boards, coolers, menu boards, and prep areas. "These trikes are heavy and can be hard on your body," Kraner tells potential employees. Each day of work means biking several miles to a downtown location and setting up the propane grill. They then prepare and sell beef, pork, chicken, and vegetarian tacos and *dillas*, as well as chips, guacamole, and salsa. Everything is made with fresh ingredients. The company's mission statement reads, "Taco Pedalers takes pride in using local and often times organic produce and meats. We support small businesses, use only compostable and biodegradable paper products, and are completely powered by pedals."

Kraner's mother, Ellen Finley, isn't remotely surprised that her daughter has created such an unusual and successful outdoor business. "My father, grandfather, and great-grandfather were all woodworkers," she said in an interview with the author. "Erika took after them. When she was young, she picked up some branches someone had cut up, added some spray paint and fishing line, and created this amazing headboard for her bed. Later, she took an old doorless refrigerator and a window and created an incredible CD-cabinet. When the bikes arrived from Mexico," added Finley, "they had nothing but a basket on the front. Erika custom designed them so that they would meet all city codes."

Like the majority of outdoor jobs, the Taco Pedalers can work only when the weather cooperates. Since Portland is known for winter rains, this means shutting down between the months of October through February. That also means that Kraner and McClure have to work that much harder during the dry, warm months of March through September. Most of the time, they work seven days a week, for ten hours a day. "Having your own business is harder than you think, but it is completely worth it," Finley told the author. "Just be passionate about whatever it is you do and take time to build it!"

Kraner and McClure found a way to combine their fondness for Mexican food with their love of being outside and riding bicycles. They also selected one of the best cities for a business like Taco Pedalers. Portland is crazy about natural, organic food, independently owned companies, and cyclists. It is the perfect combination for an outdoor job that is fun, healthy, and successful!

Do you have what it takes to make money working outdoors like Kraner and McClure? You love it outside. You would rather camp out in a tent than sleep in the softest bed. You prefer going to sleep to train whistles, wind chimes, and crickets than to music or the television. A field trip to a fish hatchery or wildlife preserve sounds far more fun than one to the museum. You don't mind the summer's heat or the winter's cold, and no rainstorm is going to send you inside. Free time is spent riding bikes, shooting baskets, playing Frisbee in the park, throwing a ball, and practicing moves on your skateboard. Now that you're older, the idea of getting a job is OK. But getting one that keeps you inside all day isn't. Is it possible to make money and stay outside the typical four walls?

It is! Read on to learn how to find outside jobs, whether you want one just for the summer months or as a full-time profession, and discover what traits you will need to succeed in such a venture. Along the way, you will meet several young people who, like Kraner and McClure, have found a way to earn a paycheck—and stay out in nature.

CHAPTER 1

'TIS THE SEASON

Ah, summer time. You have been counting down the days all the way through the dreary months of winter and the wet and muddy months of spring. Finally, the day arrives. Summer is here! School is out for what feels like forever. When you look to the future, all you can see is sunshine, relaxation, and free time.

Although you might want to spend your summer sleeping in and hanging out with friends, there is another way to put that time to use—getting a seasonal job. It gives you the chance to be outside, which you've been waiting for all year long. Yet it also allows you to earn some money, learn some new skills, meet some interesting new people, and get a better idea of what kind of career you might (or might not!) want someday.

SEASONAL WORK

Seasonal work, which typically starts right around Memorial Day and runs through Labor Day, can be the perfect first job for a teen. Such work is often available right in your hometown, depending on where you live. Do tourists commonly travel to your city, for example? Do you have amusement parks, natural scenic spots, or other attractions? These places often require extra help during the summer months. Other establishments in your city might have additional job openings during the summer, too. Jeff Allen, cofounder of Aboutjobs.com, told Katie Thomason of eHow, "Many year-round retail establishments have increased demand in the summer from increased tourism; restaurants might have expanded outdoor seating, and some stores have extended hours and need more staff."

Be sure also to look for potential jobs beyond your city or town. What attractions, resorts, or tourist spots can you find throughout your state? Don't stop there, however. Look online at job openings across the country, and then keep going—explore your options in other countries. Worldwide travel can be an amazing experience. Many reputable organizations offer work, accommodations, and travel expenses to teens willing to travel abroad for meaningful work. Some of the most common seasonal jobs include working at:

- Day or resident summer camps
- Amusement parks
- Holiday resorts and spas
- Tourist attractions
- Ranches and farms
- Tree and plant nurseries and landscaping services
- Sporting events
- Beaches
- City, state, and national parks
- Golf courses
- Agricultural farms
- Construction sites

HELPFUL STEPS

If you decide that working a seasonal job sounds like fun, there are some important tips to remember. First, do your

Working with plants is a wonderful way to stay connected with nature and the outdoors. Jobs working outside are often available during the spring and summer, plus you might find work in local nurseries with greenhouses during the off-season.

homework. Research what options you have and what kind of skills are required for each job. It is a waste of your time—and your potential employer's—to apply for a job that requires a certain skill set or certification that you don't actually have. Also, look into travel arrangements and costs. If you're working locally, your travel costs are going to be minimal, but if you have to fly to Europe, the cost can be quite substantial. Explore what the job does and does not offer. For example, if you have to live away from home while working, are food and accommodations provided, are they part of your payment, or will you have to pay for them yourself, out of your own pocket?

Second, be prepared to work long hours and many days in a row. For example, if you decide to spend the summer doing agricultural work like picking fruit, you will most likely work from dawn to dusk. This may last only for a short period, such as one to two weeks. Being in good physical shape is essential—for this job and almost every type of outdoor work. A number of these positions will require you to use muscles you didn't know you had. And, in the beginning, each one of those muscles is sure to complain.

Third, be flexible in what kind of work you are willing to do when you are originally hired. In order to get your foot in the door of an organization or company, you might initially have to let

Farm and agricultural work are great employment options for people who enjoy sunshine and fresh air. It takes a fair amount of muscles, too, so be ready to work hard!

go of the idea of working outside. Instead, you may begin to work your way up the ladder by laboring in the kitchen washing dishes, in the laundry room cleaning clothes, or even behind the snack bar serving drinks and nachos. You may also

Most farm work is down and dirty. It is very practical labor—like shoveling dirty hay out of a horse stall and replacing it with fresh. But it can also be very satisfying to both the body and soul.

find yourself doing work you hadn't imagined. Working as a camp counselor, for example, might include teaching crafts and leading night hikes. But it also might require mending tents; cleaning out cabins, dining halls, and latrines; and handling plumbing problems.

Fourth, plan ahead. If you are applying for summer work, don't wait until May to start applying. Experts suggest that you start in late winter or early spring. "As each day passes by, there will be less opportunity," Heather Boyer, director of marketing for SnagAJob.com, told Katie Thomason of eHow. Allen adds, "Application deadlines vary, but if you want a particular type of job with a specific employer, do your research now to find out when their application deadlines close so that you don't miss out on the opportunity."

Fifth, do some research regarding the job outlook for the field you are investigating. For example, the future for recreation workers, according to the *Occupational Outlook Handbook*, published by the Bureau of Labor Statistics, states that the median pay for this type of job is $10.70 per hour. The field is growing at an average of 19 percent, or about the same rate as the overall national average. Figure out how much you will make with this job. It should be minimum wage or better, unless money is taken out for food and lodging.

Finally, create a strong résumé that you can hand out, mail, e-mail, or post in response to job listings. Make sure to include any of your skills, certifications, abilities, training, and professional experience on the résumé. Also ask for letters of recommendation or reference from teachers and guidance counselors, former bosses and coworkers, and family friends. If you can speak more than one language, be sure to mention that. Also include extracurricular activities and volunteer positions.

The summer can be a wonderful opportunity to take a seasonal job. Make the most of those weeks by learning and earning!

MAKING MONEY AND LEARNING SKILLS WITH THE NORTHWEST YOUTH CORPS

Caspian wanted his first job to teach him some important skills, from how to handle power tools to how to work with a team. He also wanted to earn a paycheck while enjoying the great outdoors. He found the perfect opportunity to combine earning, learning, and outdoor adventuring in the Northwest Youth Corps (NYC). "I heard about the organization from my older sister," Caspian explained in an interview with the author. "She knew me well and thought I might like it."

Headquartered in Eugene, Oregon, NYC sends youth out on environmental projects throughout Oregon, Washington, and California. Jobs might involve clearing trails, restoring campgrounds, repairing bridges, or protecting native plants. "We also focus on invasive species removal," Elizabeth Karas, NYC's director of marketing and community relations, told the author. "That's a fancy way of saying we get rid of blackberries." In addition, participants learn basic camping skills. "They are taught how to cook and set up a tent and campsite. We are here to help counteract nature deficit disorder."

Established in 1984, NYC is based on the principles of the Civilian Conservation Corps, a Depression-era New Deal organization created by Franklin D. Roosevelt in 1933. "We started with fifty kids and two rental vans," said Karas, "and now we are averaging 1,000 kids each year and have a fleet of vans." Most of the kids involved with the program are between fourteen and nineteen, although NYC has programs for some as young as seven and for adults. "There is no experience needed to join this group," explained Karas. "You just have to show a want or a need and then apply. We have a lot of kids who have never seen the stars or gone camping, and, after being immersed in this experience, they never want to sleep in a regular bed again." Caspian was already a fan of camping when he signed up for the spring session. "I love the sounds of the forest," he said.

NYC focuses on teaching multiple skills, including leadership, community networking, empowerment, and how to cope with physical challenges. "I had to learn a lot about endurance and motivation," said Caspian. "I especially enjoyed the camaraderie between me and my team. I enjoyed laying down a trail in the forest so that people can go through and have fun without harming the wildlife. I learned that my body can handle hard work for a long time, such as lifting logs," added Caspian. "I learned how to do knots and use outdoor tools."

At the end of each program, members go home with a paycheck that has their food allotment deducted. Bonuses for working hard and sticking with the program are added. Caspian earned a paycheck and a lot more. "Whatever I do next, I know I will take what I learned about teamwork and motivation with me. NYC taught me that I can handle whatever I come up against, as well as not to panic if I am unsure what to do."

Caspian has advice for other young people who are exploring working outside and attending NYC. "Be prepared to be exhausted," he warned. "Be able to live with a group of people for weeks. You will learn to appreciate things more, like the taste of an apple after a hard day's work. Another thing to know about working outdoors—you may not have a bathroom," he added with a grin. "You just might have to dig a latrine and use something called a 'nature wipe.' My advice? Don't use poison oak—it hurts!"

OUTDOOR . . . . SCHOOL?

Imagine putting together your class schedule and having to choose between mountaineering, rock climbing, and wilderness medical school. If you're enrolled at National Outdoor Leadership School (NOLS), those just might be your options.

NOLS was established in 1965 and at first offered just three wilderness courses. One hundred young men showed up to enroll. In 1967, young women were allowed to enroll, and by 1970, NOLS had more than 750 students. In the years since then, the organization has continued to expand, offering additional classes in more and more parts of the world. It is listed as the largest backcountry permit holder in the country. It has produced more than 120,000 graduates and has operations in fourteen locations across the globe. For a number of years, NOLS has been listed as one of America's best places to work in *Outside Magazine*.

"NOLS exists to take people outside," Bruce Palmer, director of admissions and marketing, said in an interview with the author. "We focus on leadership, environmental skills, and training people to be outdoor leaders. Courses run from ten days to seventy-seven days, but the average class is one month long." Every course NOLS offers to participants earns them college credit with the University of Utah.

One of the best combinations for many young people is work that merges with travel to amazing places throughout the world. NOLS and companies like it help young people meet these twin goals.

The skills NOLS looks for in its leaders include advanced technical skills in one of the main sports (rock climbing, kayaking, skiing, etc.). Leadership candidates must also demonstrate strong communication skills and the ability to teach, plan, and expedite a course. Navigation skills are essential as well, including GPS, mapping, and compass use. Basic skills are also a priority, such as setting up a campsite and "leave no trace" camping practices. Palmer suggests that anyone who likes the outdoors and might want to pursue working for NOLS get as much experience as possible. "Join Boy Scout or Girl Scout troops that go camping," he said. "Anything that gets you outdoors is great."

CHAPTER 2

BEING YOUR OWN BOSS

Have you ever dreamed about being your own boss? Have you thought about what it would take to create your own business and work only for yourself? There are certainly benefits to self-employment and being an entrepreneur. These benefits include choosing the jobs you want. They also include turning down the jobs you don't want, working the hours and days that fit your schedule the best, setting your own fees, and not having to share the money with a boss or coworkers. There are downsides, too, of course. Self-employment means more paperwork at tax time, less free time to hang out with friends or relax, the need to develop discipline and self-motivation, and the engaging in relentless self-promotion. There is a great deal of responsibility resting on your shoulders alone. Just ask Liam!

IDENTIFYING A COMMUNITY'S NEEDS

Liam and his family moved to Oregon a few months ago. Moving is a familiar process for all of them. At only fourteen years old, Liam has already lived in Arizona, California, Michigan, and Illinois. Since his family was often struggling to make ends meet, when Liam wanted to join Boy Scouts, the money just wasn't there. "He joined Scouts around his sixth birthday," his mother, Kathleen, remembered in an interview with the author. Liam paid his own way by becoming one of the top five popcorn sellers in the entire district. He sold enough kernels to cover the cost of his uniforms, fees, gear, and even summer camp.

Making the most of the seasons where you live is another way to make money. You might live where snow needs to be shoveled in the winter months, whereas others might live where yards need to be mowed year-round. Use your climate to your advantage when looking for work ideas.

"Next, he started brainstorming," said Kathleen. Liam was too young to babysit or dog walk, but he wanted to do something to earn money and help his family. "I made up business cards and fliers on the computer for my business, 'Just Ask

Liam,'" he told the author, "and I offered to take people's trash cans out to the curb the night before trash collection for $1." As he got older, Liam discovered other ways to make money in whatever neighborhood his family was currently living. One area had a lot of older residents, so he took in their groceries, weeded their gardens, and shoveled snow from their driveways. "I recycled for the neighborhood, too," added Liam. "I would go to people's houses and collect their aluminum and other recyclables, and then turn them in for whatever money I could get."

At eight, Liam took first aid and lifesaving courses with the Red Cross. "I did that for a few reasons," he explained. "It was part of earning a Boy Scout badge, plus I tend to be a bit accident-prone, so it was for my own benefit, too." He was hired as a mother's helper for some busy moms and also helped a woman with a feral cat program she was organizing. "I helped her catch the cats and feed them," Liam said. "I also helped make beds for the cats and prepare the shelter for the winter months." By this time, Liam was making at least $30 a week and over $100 a week in the spring.

Each time Liam's family moved, he would walk through his new neighborhood and "scope out the area." "I would look at the houses and see what people might need," he explained. "What services do they need done, but don't want to do? If you figure that out, find out the going rate for those services, and then charge slightly less, you will find work." Over the years, Liam has helped with construction, hauled trash to Dumpsters, walked dogs, watched children, and worked at local market booths on weekends. "He doesn't like making less than $40 a week," said Kathleen. "He just received a new batch of business cards and is about to start handing them out everywhere he can!"

Liam doesn't plan to work outside all of his life; he has plans to go to a culinary academy and become a combination chef and personal fitness trainer. In the meantime, he is learning skills, meeting people, earning money, and enjoying the outdoors—not a bad combination for an industrious fourteen-year-old!

Being Your Own Boss

SCOPING OUT THE NEIGHBORHOOD

If you want to start your own business and become an entrepreneur like Liam, a great place to start is exploring the area where you live to see what services might be needed. If you are surrounded by apartment buildings, lawn care might not be the best choice. If you live in the South, snow shoveling is probably out of the question. If you have retirement homes or senior care facilities on either side, babysitting is not a likely option. What do you think the people around you might need the most?

Some of the most common types of self-employment jobs for young people include:

- Washing cars
- Mowing lawns
- Doing yard work

Strong back muscles, patience, and a love for sports can sometimes blend together. When caddying, you might even learn a few tips to improve your own swing!

23

- Babysitting children
- Walking pets
- Making repairs
- Holding yard sales
- Teaching outdoor skills
- Coaching sports
- Tuning bicycles
- Assisting with birthday parties
- Being a golf caddy
- Delivering newspapers
- Manning local market booths
- Weeding and watering gardens
- Lifeguarding at local pools, lakes, etc.
- Working at a day camp
- Selling home party supplies
- Delivering messages or documents by bicycle or on foot

As you look through this list or one you come up with yourself, ask yourself the following questions:

1. *Which of these services do I think would fit in best with the area where I live?* Look at the houses—do any need lawn services? Pool care? Painting?

2. *What skills do these jobs require? Do they require skills that I already have or do I need to learn something additional? If I do, where can I find classes, workshops, or internships to teach these skills?* If you are competent at a skill, teaching it to others is wonderful, but be sure not to oversell yourself. Just because you beat your dad at chess every night does not mean you are able to teach young people how to win chess competitions. If you attended a day camp last summer, you are not necessarily prepared and qualified to be a counselor this summer.

Raking leaves is a chore that has been performed for countless generations. If you know someone in your neighborhood who could use some help with the job, you might have found the perfect way to make some money.

3. *How can I demonstrate to potential clients that I am professional and reliable? What certifications or training should I have to show to them?* If you are certified in first aid, for example, carry the card on you to show to potential customers. If you have earned a food handler's card, put it in your wallet to show you've done your homework!

HELPING THE COMMUNITY

When Jacob was only five years old, he already knew he loved the outdoors. He joined Jane Goodall's Roots and Shoots program. Eleven years later, he became one of their youth leaders. When he recently took a week-long summer class, Jacob discovered that the only thing he loved as much as the outdoors was making movies. The local city council was looking for young people to make a documentary about the Columbia River slough. This is an area in Oregon where the water drains into a stream and eventually into the Willamette River. Jacob joined the project and has been learning a great deal about the outdoors, the environment, and the art of filmmaking.

Jacob and his family are also a part of the Resources for Health organization's Wheel Solution program. Every Wednesday, Jacob and his family stop by the local farmers' market to load up on whatever fresh fruits and vegetables are in season. Next, they deliver the produce to area residents. "I like seeing how enthusiastic people are with the fresh farm food and getting to know the people I'm delivering to," Jacob said in an interview with the author.

In addition to these two projects, Jacob is a volunteer for Oregon's Nature Park Interpretive Center. He usually works with kids ages four through eleven years old. "Volunteering is a good place to start a career outdoors," he added. "I'm certain that most of my talents and interests have been influenced by my interaction with nature and outdoor activities." Jacob hopes to find a way to blend his fascination for film with his passion for nature. He advises other young people to "get experience, make connections, and enjoy what they're doing. Also be patient because opportunities manifest when given time."

4. *How much time do I want to dedicate to this job? How many hours per day and which days? Weekdays and/or weekends?* Remember, you will have to work around school hours, extracurricular requirements, and family obligations.

5. *Do I need any kind of insurance coverage for the jobs I am offering? If so, where do I find it?* Talk to your parents or a lawyer about whether or not you need to provide insurance coverage for the job you want to begin. If you're going to coach children's tennis, for example, what happens if someone gets hurt? You will need to know what insurance coverage exists and what you are legally required to carry.

6. *What kind of marketing and promotion do I need to do? Will I need flyers and business cards? If so, can I make them myself? Where should I post them? Should I use digital and social media to advertise my services?* Ask family and friends to help get the word out by handing out printed materials and forwarding and posting digital ad content. Check with local merchants as they are often open to promoting small businesses (just make sure your service isn't in competition with theirs). Post fliers on supermarket and public library or town hall bulletin boards, town center kiosks, and other places where people stop and look.

Answering all of these questions carefully and thoroughly is a vital part of your business plan. If you want your particular service—whether it is mowing lawns or washing cars—to become an actual business, and not just something you do here and there as a hobby in order to make a few dollars, then you need to design a workable business plan. Being an entrepreneur is fun—but demanding. No one else is going to promote or

Open air, farmers', and Saturday markets are great places to find seasonal work. Whether you are helping people pick the ripest peaches or selling the handmade crafts your aunt makes, it can provide valuable experience in customer service.

advertise your services. It is up to you to network and reach out to people in a professional way. Remember that the impression you make on people with the way you speak, look, and behave is going to help sway them to hire you—or to look elsewhere. So talk, dress, and act responsibly!

MEET THREE TEENAGE ENTREPRENEURS

Creating your own business may sound exciting—and intimidating. Here are three young women who rose to the challenge.

Madison (age fifteen) was inspired to start working for the same reason many people are—she wanted the money to buy something. In her case, it was a camera because she is interested in photography. She also likes dogs, so she started advertising a dog-walking business. She posted fliers throughout her neighborhood and waited. Finally, a woman called and asked Madison to walk

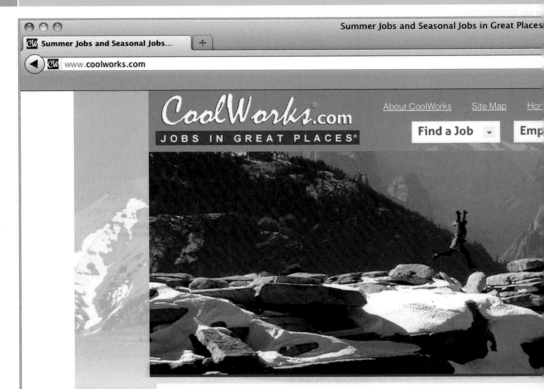

CW Summer Jobs and Seasonal Jobs...   +

www.coolworks.com

CoolWorks.com

JOBS IN GREAT PLACES ®

Find job postings and employer profiles for your next work adventure.

What's New	Jobs by Category
Help Wanted Now	Jobs by State
Highlighted Jobs	National Park Jobs
Careers	Jobs by Season
Seasonal Professionals	Jobs Map
	U.S. Work Visa Info

Newest Job Postings

Wait Staff Positions at a Progressive Waterfront Restaurant

CoolWorks (www.coolworks.com) is one of many Web sites that advertises amazing jobs for young and adventurous people available throughout the world. Check out its "What's New" and "Highlighted Jobs" on a regular basis.

HELP WANTED NOW

Harley, a golden retriever. Madison enjoyed being with the dog and earning money, but walking in the rain and mud wasn't as much fun. "Working outside has taught me that I do not want to sit in an office all day long," Madison said in an interview with the author. "The job has also taught me the importance of wearing good shoes and being truthful." Currently, she is searching for a few more dogs to join Harley.

Kaylee (fourteen) loves being outside and found the perfect training ground and workplace through Trackers Earth, a school that teaches survival skills and arts. She took a class, became a teaching assistant, and then a counselor-in-training. "We are like a family that works together to take care of all aspects of our daily life, while teaching kids how to fish, build fires, weave baskets, cook on a rocket stove outdoors, gather wild edibles, carve wood with knives, and sneak silently through the woods," Kaylee explained to the author. "My love of wild things and the willingness of the staff to teach me what they knew inspired me to join. Trackers is my second family. They encourage and coach me to grow and develop as, hopefully, a future staff member."

During her experience with Trackers, Kaylee has learned a great deal. "I've learned to bring up a fire from a mere coal, to sit still and quiet in the woods, listening to the calls of the birds to tell me if someone is near," she said. "I've learned how to hide myself, to remain completely unseen in the shadows. I've learned to weave and spin. . . I have developed a repertoire of survival skills that make me feel confident in going out in the wild." Kaylee hopes to keep working with kids. In the meantime, she advises other young people who want to work outdoors to start by overcoming adversity. "To become an outdoor teacher, you have to release your death grip on the modern world. Nobody can stay inside forever . . . Being an outdoor teacher gets your creative juices flowing and more learning takes place!"

Livia (sixteen) started providing henna tattoos to summer campers in Idaho. When camp was over, she came home, bought a kit, and started practicing on anyone who would sit still. Finally, she became a vendor at her city's farmers' market. "At that point, I just wanted to be able to cover the cost of renting the space, and anything above that was just icing on the cake," Livia explained to the author. "I was in it for the experience and the fun, not to make money." The henna went well—soon she was being called to do parties and other events. Knowing what to charge was challenging, so Livia researched pricing online and went to other area markets to see what artists were charging. "You have to be really persistent, as there have been days where I only net $4, and other times where I net $150," she explained. "It's always hard to predict whether

I'll be busy on market day, because it depends on the weather, if people are on vacation, and countless other factors that I'm not aware of and are unpredictable."

Although henna can be done indoors, Livia definitely prefers outdoors. "At the market, it is noisy and sunny and windy, and there's more of a festive atmosphere, which just makes it generally more enjoyable." Has working at the market changed how Livia sees her future? "Doing tattoos has shown me how to go through the process of applying for something, as well as making a résumé, and negotiating business with people who are always much older than me," she said.

CHAPTER 3

LEARNING THROUGH INTERNSHIPS

Have you ever followed someone around to learn how that person did something? It might have been an older brother showing off his skateboard tricks or a sister practicing her paint strokes. It could have been a parent cooking dinner, a friend playing guitar, or a neighbor building a shed. Shadowing or watching someone who is skilled at something is a wonderful way to learn, and this kind of observation, imitation, and apprenticeship can be performed in a number of outdoor summer jobs. It is also a process that dates all the way back to medieval times, when young people worked as apprentices to skilled craftsmen.

During your summer months, give some thought to applying to an internship program. It gives you a chance to learn a profession up close and personal. You get the chance to ask questions and explore different career avenues. In some cases, you might even get paid. Internships also allow you to network with people working within the field that interests you. They give you the chance to find out if the job you had imagined is anything like the reality of the day-to-day work.

FINDING AN INTERNSHIP THAT IS RIGHT FOR YOU

Some of the outdoor jobs that are frequently held by young interns (and that can eventually develop into careers) include:

Shadowing is one of the best ways to learn some basic skills. If you want to know more about automotive work, for example, ask if you can intern at a local repair shop. Hands-on experience can be the fastest way to learn and the best way to impress potential employers.

- Construction workers
- Pest control workers
- Brick masons
- Fishery workers
- Carpenters
- Roofers
- Welders

Reading textbooks, watching videos, and surfing Web sites are all good ways to learn, but with some trades, such as construction, it is hard to beat putting your practical skills to use right at the work site!

Finding a place to work as an intern may be as easy as asking your mom or dad to look into the teen job opportunities where they work, exploring options with your guidance counselor, or talking to your neighbors and family friends. Other times, you may have to apply for an internship, which traditionally includes submitting a résumé and being interviewed. You should give each one of these steps the same focus and thoroughness that you would those of any other job application process.

Internships come in all sizes and shapes. They typically last for two to three months. If you're not sure where to start when exploring this employment avenue, check out the "Internship Predictor" at Internships.com. It can help you tailor your interests and preferences to the internships that are available. You can also search online to see what is available. When you do, be sure to put in the most precise search words you can (e.g., "communication internships" will not be as helpful as "student summer publishing internship Seattle Washington"). Some internships are paid, offering hourly or weekly wages or a stipend. Other internships are unpaid. It is often the case that the most popular fields and industries—such as television, film, fashion, magazine publishing, and communications/public relations—are unpaid. This is because there are so many young people willing to work for free in these industries while gaining valuable professional experience and networking opportunities. Some unpaid

ADVICE FROM INTERNSHIPS.COM

According to Colleen Sabitano, the intern coach at Internships.com, the role of the intern within a business is changing. This needs to be reflected in your approach when you go in for an interview. "When asked in an interview, 'Why do you want this internship?' focus on what you can do for the employer. Do not talk about how this is a great opportunity for you to learn about the industry and profession," Sabitano advises on Internships.com. "While that also might be true, it is not the most important reason to highlight in the interview. What's important to the employer is your ability to take initiative and produce quality work as a member of their team."

internships, however, may offer course credit for school. It is up to you to research these issues, and if you can't find the answer, ask! After all, asking questions to discover answers is what internships are all about.

FROM INTERN TO EMPLOYEE

Dimitri (age twenty-three) knew that he wanted a job that would allow him to make money, did not involve a desk, and made it possible to travel around and see the world. He discovered it—surprisingly—through welding. After earning his two-year degree in welding, Dimitri was hired as a welder/fitter and was taught advanced skills and techniques while on the job. This position is much like a traditional paid internship.

Learning to weld has been challenging. According to Dimitri, the most difficult part is "learning to stand like a statue and move with vegetable slowness and mechanical precision. Some welds can be ruined if you breathe wrong," he explained in an interview with the author. "Only surgeons have steadier hands than ours." Dimitri hopes to follow his welding internship with a stint working on ships at sea. "I simply like ships," he said.

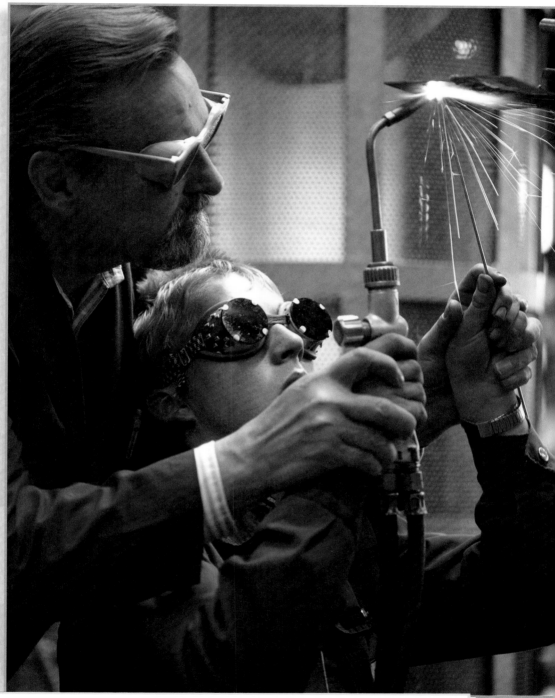

Nothing makes a job more real than seeing it up close and in progress. Internships and shadowing allow you the chance to do that and explore if you truly have an interest in and aptitude for a given career path.

"Building ships and maybe being part of the onboard maintenance crew would be so rewarding."

In the meantime, Dimitri has some advice for other young people. "Be a good judge of your comfort zones," he said. "Working in a shop pays less than working in the field, but think about wearing heavy, protective clothing and working over metal that radiates heat like an oven under the summer sun. Also, be versatile—the more you can do, the more you are worth, and the more fun you can have. Finally, be safe—do what it takes to go home with all your extremities, even if it means going home without the job."

CHAPTER 4

THE POWER OF VOLUNTEERING

If you want to spend your time outdoors earning an income, that is certainly understandable. But don't overlook the personal, professional, and social opportunities and benefits that volunteering offers. Volunteering is incredibly enriching for the individual and the community, even though no paychecks are involved.

Teen volunteering is growing throughout the country. According to the Corporation for National and Community Service, volunteering among sixteen- to nineteen-year-olds more than doubled between 1989 and 2005. Why are so many teenagers giving up their free time and opportunities to make money in order to volunteer instead? In addition to being motivated by compassion and a desire to help their community, these teens have also realized that volunteering gives them the chance to acquire many personal and professional advantages. Let's explore a few of them. Volunteering can:

- Give you valuable work experience that future employers will respect
- Help you learn to work with other people and be a part of a team
- Connect you with people and organizations that you might network with and/or work for in the future
- Introduce you to new careers you hadn't considered before
- Demonstrate which jobs you enjoy and which you don't
- Teach you skills like decision making and time management

Volunteering is a win-win situation because everyone benefits. You learn new skills and meet new people, the organization gets your much-needed help, and the community is assisted and enriched.

- Enhance your résumé for future jobs and your application for college admissions and/or scholarships

PLACES TO VOLUNTEER

OK—you're sold! The idea of volunteering appeals to you and you recognize all the opportunities it might bring. The next step is figuring out what kind of volunteer work you wish to provide and for what kind of organization. Here are some resources to help zero in on your ideal volunteer position. Many of these can involve at least some outdoor work. Start by looking locally. You can talk with your guidance counselor or other staff at school to see if they are aware of volunteer requests. Some of the organizations that often seek young volunteers include:

- Nursing homes (reading out loud, leading games)
- Senior centers (teaching computer skills)
- City parks (clean up or trail building)
- Community gardens and nurseries (weeding, watering)
- Boys' Club/Girls' Club (helping with homework, leading games)
- City tour groups (showing city sites, answering questions)
- Museums and aquariums (helping with displays, leading tours, staffing the gift shop)
- Churches (teaching, cleaning, babysitting)
- Hospitals (delivering flowers, working in the gift shop)

- Public libraries (summer reading and literacy programs, storytelling)
- Performing arts theaters (ushering, helping with props and scenery)
- Community centers and local YMCAs (teaching classes, coaching, leading field trips)

Volunteering opportunities are found throughout your community, so take a close look around and see what organizations, groups, churches, and other people might need and appreciate your time, energy, and know-how.

- Animal shelters (walking dogs, cleaning cages and kennels)
- Local cable access stations (running errands)
- Recycling centers or thrift stores (organizing donations, taking payments)
- Local day camps (helping with games and other activities)
- Public and private schools (tutoring)

A number of local organizations often need volunteers. Check out the local branch of the Red Cross, for example. Check to see if your area has a search and rescue team. Go online to visit Habitat for Humanity and see if there are any projects planned in your area.

Draft a résumé and then go to these organizations in person. You may be asked to drop off your information or schedule a time for a face-to-face interview. Of course, you should also be ready to explain, off the top of your head, why you want to volunteer. You should genuinely believe in and be committed to the work being done by the organization for which you hope to volunteer. The services that these organizations provide are so important that they don't want to take on teens whose only interest in the work is to polish their college applications and résumés.

TAKE IT SERIOUSLY!

As a person donating your free time, energy, and skills, it might be easy for you not to take your volunteer job seriously. If there's no time clock and no paycheck, what is the harm in skipping a day here and there, right? Wrong. You are establishing a work record and a reputation for your future. People are relying on your presence and hard work. Commit to showing up when and where you are expected. Give your volunteer position as much dedication and effort as you would a paying job because you never know who is watching and taking note of your stellar qualities—or lack thereof.

WORKING WITH SEARCH AND RESCUE

Imagine searching the base of a mountain, along darkened trails, or through dense forest for a hiker who is missing. If you are part of a search and rescue (SAR) team, that might be exactly what you're doing. A number of SAR teams rely on teen volunteers to help them when a person goes missing. Coogan (age sixteen) joined SAR a year ago and fell in love with it. "It's hard and tiring and exhausting, but I still love it," he said in an interview with the author. "Ninety-nine percent of the time we are outside, and it is cold and wet, but I love working outside. It is one of the best places to be."

Through his training with SAR, Coogan has learned how to perform first aid and CPR, use a portable defibrillator (a device that can normalize the rhythm of a human heart in emergency situations). He has been trained to navigate by compass or map; construct a shelter that can withstand rain, wind, and snow; and build a fire that can burn all night. "I have also learned not to lean against small trees—they might fall," he said. "Also, listen. If you don't listen to your teammates, you or someone else could get injured."

When his time with SAR is over, Coogan is planning on joining fire and rescue. For other young people who might be interested in joining their local SAR team, Coogan has some advice. "Be prepared—this isn't easy—it is hard work. Know that when you are out there on a search, you are saving someone's life, not goofing off with friends. If you choose to join SAR, I want you to be prepared to have some of the best years of your life," he added. "You'll make friends fast, and they will help you through it all."

HELPING HABITAT

Ever since 1976, Habitat for Humanity (H4H), a nonprofit organization, has helped build more than 500,000 homes across the country. This group depends largely on volunteers for its outdoor projects and offers programs for young children, teenagers, and young adults. One volunteer, Nicole (age twenty-one), saw H4H as offering the perfect combination to satisfy her passion for both the outdoors and for hard and meaningful work. "My parents told me over and over again that the best way to get a job is to volunteer first," she said in an interview with the author. "So, I strapped on a tool belt, bought my own hammer to make me feel official, and walked onto my first H4H construction site."

The work was far from easy. "Crawling underneath a house with a ventilator over your mouth and goggles over your eyes to install insulation with a nail gun is NOT fun," she admitted. What was fun for Nicole, however, was working outside and being part of a team. "I'm a sucker for camaraderie," she explained. "No matter how hard the work is, if you've got people who are laughing, joking, and suffering along with you, the job is nothing. Habitat gives you a glimpse of people trusting you in an age where you aren't always given trust. For me, it was a chance to prove myself TO myself."

Habitat for Humanity is an organization that has helped countless families move into their own homes. Volunteering for it can teach you how to use a variety of building and power tools and construction techniques. It also helps you make the world a far better place for individuals, families, and entire communities.

After her time with H4H, Nicole went on to two years in search and rescue, and then to six months working on a tourist train in Alaska. Next, she led field trips for a local community center. Currently, she is preparing for a six-month exploration of the exotic Australian Outback. She hopes all young people know that working outdoors may not be easy, but it is always worth it. "What helps is having a goal," she said. "Traveling is what I want to do and what I want to BE. When you have a dream as fierce as that, everything else is small fish!"

CHAPTER 5

THE BUSINESS PART OF WORK

Now, let's turn to the business aspect of getting a job outdoors, including relevant laws, record keeping, and paperwork. You need to be familiar with a variety of numbers, including how many hours you are allowed to work at what age, how much to charge for your work, and what income must be reported to Uncle Sam.

You might recall from history classes that long ago, there were no laws regarding how many hours or what kind of jobs minors could have. That might sound like a lot of freedom, but it was just the opposite. Until child labor laws were developed, even very young children could be put to work for forty hours or more a week. It was a cruel practice that severely harmed a lot of young people, so the government stepped in and developed some guidelines. How do they apply to you today?

Today's child labor laws are designed to strike a balance between the interests and desires of industrious teens and the necessary protections that will prevent exploitation of young workers. Careful limits are placed on the amount of hours teens can work on what days and in what times of the year, the types of workplace, and the working conditions. All of this is meant to protect the freedoms of teens who wish to work while helping to guarantee that that work will be safe and gratifying, will pay fairly, and will not infringe upon or detract from their schooling.

Child labor laws have made the world a safer, happier place in which to grow up. You might feel limited by the laws telling you where, when, and how you can work. But if you take a closer look, you will find these laws are keeping you safe from harm and exploitation and protecting your best interests.

FEDERAL CHILD LABOR LAWS

Where and how much you can work is based on three main factors: your age, if school is in session, and how dangerous the work is. Take a look at the chart of these general national guidelines below and see which category fits you the best. Keep in mind that individual states also have their own rules about working.

AGE	HOURS PERMITTED	TYPES OF JOBS
Under 14 years old		Deliver newspapers Babysit Act/perform in movies, TV, or theater Family-owned business
14–15 years old	3 hours or less/school days 18 hours or less/week when school is in session 8 hours or less/day when school is out 40 hours or less/week when school is out Only between the hours 7 a.m. to 7 p.m. on any day except when school is out, and then it extends to 9 p.m.	Retail jobs Computer work Errands/delivery Pumping gas/washing cars Food service/limited cooking Lifeguarding/amusement parks Yard work without power-driven equipment
16–17 years old	No limitations	Any job that has not been declared hazardous* by the secretary of labor
18+ years old	No limitations	No limitations

THE IMPORTANCE OF BEING ETHICAL

You already know how important it is to be honest in your personal relationships and in school. Remember to carry that ethic over into all of your business dealings. If you're self-employed, be honest with your customers. If you say you will do something, follow through. If you make a mistake, admit it and find a way to fix it. Don't oversell your abilities. Be willing to say, "I don't know how to do that—but I can learn." Set fair and reasonable prices and stick to them. Be honest with the government about what money you made and pay what you owe in taxes. The money raised by taxes benefits all Americans, yourself included.

If you're working for a company or organization, ethics are still paramount. Be honest and fair with your superiors, your coworkers, and those who work under you. You are learning and establishing work habits that you will carry with you for the rest of your life, so start off with an unshakable commitment to integrity and truthfulness.

Remember, ethics are important in all parts of your life—work, school, home, and volunteering. Bosses should treat their workers fairly and with respect, and employees should return the favor by working hard and with honesty.

53

*What qualifies as hazardous?** According to the secretary of labor, anyone under the age of eighteen is banned from clearly dangerous actions and activities. This includes manufacturing/storing explosives, coal mining, using hazardous machines (like balers, compactors, or tools such as circular saws, chain saws, or wood chippers). If you're under eighteen, you will have to wait to get a job that involves these activities and equipment. You will also be excluded from jobs in demolition, roofing, or excavating.

PAYING THE IRS

If you haven't heard the old adage yet, here it is: the only inevitable parts of life are death and taxes. How much you will have to pay to Uncle Sam each year depends on many factors. There is a strong chance that you will not owe anything. If you are listed as a dependent on your parents' taxes and earn less than the standard deduction of about $5,750 in the previous year, for example, you don't have to file a tax return. What if you have your own business though? "There is no special tax treatment for teenagers running their own business," Carol Topp, an accountant and the founder of Teens and Taxes told Fox Business. "If you make a profit of more than $400, you must pay self-employment."

Eve Davis, licensed tax consultant and president of In and Out Taxes in Portland, Oregon, agrees. "There are legal ramifications to not reporting your income. There is interest, plus penalties for late payments that can run as high as 50 percent of the self-employment tax," she explained in an interview with the author. In addition, there is a penalty for not filing at all. "If you wait for more than three years," explained Davis, "even if you were due a refund, you won't be able to get it." Davis's bottom line advice is, "If your employer does not withhold any taxes, consult a tax professional. That way you will not make any mistakes that could later cost you money!"

SCHEDULE C
(Form 1040)

Department of the Treasury
Internal Revenue Service (99)

Profit or Loss From Business
(Sole Proprietorship)

▶ For information on Schedule C and its instructions, go to *www.irs.gov/schedulec*
▶ Attach to Form 1040, 1040NR, or 1041; partnerships generally must file Form 1065.

OMB No. 1545-0074

2011

Attachment
Sequence No. **09**

Name of proprietor	Social security number (SSN)

A	Principal business or profession, including product or service (see instructions)	**B** Enter code from instructions ▶
C	Business name. If no separate business name, leave blank.	**D** Employer ID number (EIN), (see instr.)
E	Business address (including suite or room no.) ▶	
	City, town or post office, state, and ZIP code	

F Accounting method: **(1)** ☐ Cash **(2)** ☐ Accrual **(3)** ☐ Other (specify) ▶ _____

G Did you "materially participate" in the operation of this business during 2011? If "No," see instructions for limit on losses . ☐ Yes ☐ No

H If you started or acquired this business during 2011, check here . . . . ▶ ☐

I Did you make any payments in 2011 that would require you to file Form(s) 1099? (see instructions) . . . . ☐ Yes ☐ No

J If "Yes," did you or will you file all required Forms 1099? . . . . ☐ Yes ☐ No

Part I Income

1a	Merchant card and third party payments. For 2011, enter -0- . . .	**1a**		
b	Gross receipts or sales not entered on line 1a (see instructions) . .	**1b**		
c	Income reported to you on Form W-2 if the "Statutory Employee" box on that form was checked. **Caution.** See instr. before completing this line	**1c**		
d	**Total gross receipts.** Add lines 1a through 1c	**1d**		
2	Returns and allowances plus any other adjustments (see instructions) . . .	**2**		
3	Subtract line 2 from line 1d	**3**		
4	Cost of goods sold (from line 42)	**4**		
5	**Gross profit.** Subtract line 4 from line 3	**5**		
6	Other income, including federal and state gasoline or fuel tax credit or refund (see instructions)	**6**		
7	**Gross income.** Add lines 5 and 6 . . . . ▶	**7**		

Part II Expenses   Enter expenses for business use of your home only on line 30.

8	Advertising	**8**		**18**	Office expense (see instructions)	**18**
9	Car and truck expenses (see instructions)	**9**		**19**	Pension and profit-sharing plans .	**19**
				20	Rent or lease (see instructions):	
10	Commissions and fees .	**10**		**a**	Vehicles, machinery, and equipment	**20a**
11	Contract labor (see instructions)	**11**		**b**	Other business property . . .	**20b**
12	Depletion	**12**		**21**	Repairs and maintenance . . .	**21**
13	Depreciation and section 179 expense deduction (not included in Part III) (see instructions)	**13**		**22**	Supplies (not included in Part III) .	**22**
				23	Taxes and licenses	**23**
				24	Travel, meals, and entertainment:	
14	Employee benefit programs (other than on line 19) . .	**14**		**a**	Travel	**24a**
15	Insurance (other than health)	**15**		**b**	Deductible meals and entertainment (see instructions) .	**24b**
16	Interest:			**25**	Utilities	**25**
a	Mortgage (paid to banks, etc.)	**16a**		**26**	Wages (less employment credits) .	**26**
b	Other	**16b**		**27a**	Other expenses (from line 48) . .	**27a**
17	Legal and professional services	**17**		**b**	Reserved for future use . . .	**27b**

28	**Total expenses** before expenses for business use of home. Add lines 8 through 27a . . . . . . ▶	**28**	
29	Tentative profit or (loss). Subtract line 28 from line 7	**29**	
30	Expenses for business use of your home. Attach **Form 8829**. Do **not** report such expenses elsewhere . .	**30**	
31	**Net profit or (loss).** Subtract line 30 from line 29.		
	• If a profit, enter on both **Form 1040, line 12** (or **Form 1040NR, line 13**) and on **Schedule SE, line 2.** If you entered an amount on line 1c, see instr. Estates and trusts, enter on **Form 1041, line 3.** • If a loss, you **must** go to line 32.	**31**	
32	If you have a loss, check the box that describes your investment in this activity (see instructions).		
	• If you checked 32a, enter the loss on both **Form 1040, line 12,** (or **Form 1040NR, line 13**) and on **Schedule SE, line 2.** If you entered an amount on line 1c, see the instructions for line 31. Estates and trusts, enter on **Form 1041, line 3.** • If you checked 32b, you **must** attach **Form 6198.** Your loss may be limited.	**32a** ☐ All investment is at risk. **32b** ☐ Some investment is not at risk.	

For Paperwork Reduction Act Notice, see your tax return instructions.   Cat. No. 11334P   Schedule C (Form 1040) 2011

There is a reason that people say that the only inevitable parts of life are death and taxes. If you are employed, you will have to learn about taxes. Start getting familiar with the laws and forms now, and you will be a step ahead when you get that first paycheck and face your first income tax filing.

If you are self-employed, it is essential that you remember to keep accurate, detailed records of how much you make and what business expenses and deductions (supplies, dues, equipment, advertising, etc.) you might require for your job. You will report this information on the IRS form Schedule C Profit and Loss Business form. When you are an entrepreneur with your own business, it can be a shock to discover that you have to pay self-employment tax. This tax takes a little over 15 percent of your profit.

CHAPTER
6
TAKING IT INTO THE FUTURE

Y ou have spent the summer months working outdoors. You've got dark tan lines, your callouses have callouses, and you have rock hard biceps. Perhaps you spent that time in an internship working at a national tourist attraction or holding a part-time job with the local parks and recreation department. You might have started your own business as a bicycle courier or helped your family at their market booth selling homemade bread and pastries.

No matter how you spent those hours, you will soon reach a point where you will have to ask yourself—what next? What do I do with all of this work experience? Great question! Answering, however, requires asking a few more questions.

1. *Have you enjoyed all of the time you have spent outside?* This may seem like a silly question, but you may have discovered that being out in whatever conditions nature chooses to serve up—including everything from mosquitoes and humidity to frozen fingertips and bitter wind—is not the right career path for you. If you didn't like the experience, chances are you need to start looking in another direction, possibly indoors.

2. *If you started your own business, do you plan to continue it?* The answer to this question probably depends on many factors: Did your business succeed? Did you enjoy it? Is there an ongoing market for it? Do you have the time, energy, and desire to

pursue it? If the answers are yes to these questions, you know where to look next. If the answers are no, it is time to investigate other options.

3. *Do you plan to go to college?* If the answer to this question is no, you need to decide how you want to funnel your passion for being outdoors into a job that does not require a college degree. This may involve additional internships or apprenticeships; some coursework at a trade, technical, or community college; or the creation of your own company. Blake Boles, author of *Better than College: How to Build a Successful Life without a Four-Year Degree*, suggests that young people who aren't going to college instead pursue the concept of "self-directed learning." He explained to the *Huffington Post*, "Instead of taking full-time classes, self-directed learners give themselves assignments that they find interesting, eye-opening, and challenging. They start businesses, find internships, travel the world, read and write about things that fascinate them, and work for organizations they admire." If the answer to this

Working outdoors can be hard—but it can also be a lot of fun. That doesn't mean it is the right career path for everyone, of course. After you've had some time to experience outdoor work, you can make a more educated and informed decision about what future direction you wish to take.

question is yes, however, you need to explore which colleges offer some of the best outdoor career options. You also must learn how to translate your outside work experience into a college and/or scholarship application that will get the attention of the admissions department.

One way to share your passion for outdoor work is to take a job that involves teaching skills or nature facts to other young people, as this U.S. Parks Service ranger is doing.

ASKING THE EXPERTS

Gen and Kelly Tanabe are the founders of SuperCollege, as well as the authors of fourteen books, including *Get into Any College*. They are experts on how to apply for and receive college scholarships and believe that kids who work out-

doors learn many essential skills. "Students who work outdoors learn myriad skills that would be applicable to college applications," Kelly Tanabe said in an interview with the author. "They learn how to work independently, a skill that is necessary not only for completing the applications but also for succeeding in college. Unlike traditional jobs, outdoor jobs often offer students the ability to work on their own without direct oversight from a manager. This encourages them to work independently," added Tanabe.

Students who spend time working outside also gain a hands-on understanding of the sciences, such as biology, chemistry, botany, and environmental science. "Certainly, students also learn creative problem solving because nature doesn't always behave the way that you think it would," Tanabe added. "Colleges seek students who have a passion for an area because they know that students will carry over this passion into their studies and future career." Tanabe believes that colleges appreciate students who show a respect for nature and environmentalism. "Colleges themselves are increasingly building green buildings and developing recycling programs, which

CHECK OUT THESE COLLEGES

Gen and Kelly Tanabe recommend the following colleges for those interested in outdoor careers:

- University of Colorado–Boulder
- University of Colorado–Denver
- University of Washington
- Colorado State
- Reed College
- University of California at Santa Cruz
- Middlebury College
- Montana State University
- Lewis & Clark College
- Alaska Pacific University
- University of Oregon
- Northern Arizona University

Why not combine your passion for nature with a college education? Many colleges offer some wonderful programs that can help you earn a degree while doing a lot of work and study outside.

means that they seek students who will contribute to their efforts," she stated.

"When students have an outdoor experience that they enjoy before college, it can help guide them to select a college that is an outdoors-oriented location," Tanabe went on to explain. "They may choose a college that allows them to hike, snowboard, or mountain bike over one that is an urban location. Students may also select a college that has an outdoors program. After their outdoors experience, students may find that they want to study an area that is related to the outdoors, which will also guide their college selection."

When asked what young people can possibly do to make the most of their outdoor experiences if they're going to college, Tanabe replied, "Students should try to hold as many responsibilities as possible, hold a leadership position if possible, and take initiative on projects. Leadership is a quality that colleges seek in accepting students."

The time you spend under the sun and the stars will always be a part of your life. Whether you use it to pursue a full-time career, develop your own entrepreneurial company, have fun and foster hobbies—or you decide that you much prefer working inside four walls rather than outside them—it will not be time wasted. Mother Nature has a lot to offer, and you can find the best possible way to connect with her through an investment of time, persistence, and dedication.

GETTING HIRED

Wondering what it takes to get hired at a camp or other outdoor organization? According to Tony Deis, the founder of Trackers Earth in Oregon and California, it requires a great deal of time spent in the field. "Experience is—hands-down—what gets you hired," he said in an interview with the author. "There are other important skills that you can develop, of course, but field experience is the key."

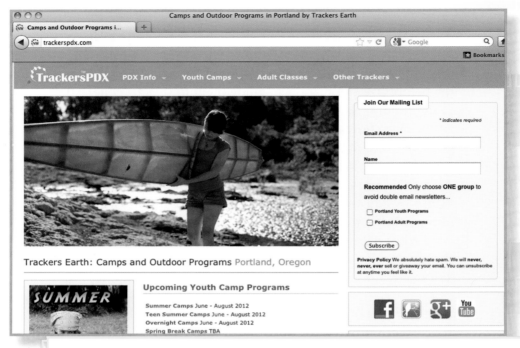

Trackers Earth (www.trackersearth.com) offers the best of all worlds—teaching teens about the outdoor world while also offering young adults the internships and jobs of a lifetime.

Trackers Earth was established in 2004 and is largely based on Deis's work with the Audubon Society of Portland, Metro Parks, Greenspaces, and Portland State University. Over the last ten years, Trackers Earth has become one of the largest and most successful summer camps and outdoor programs in Oregon. As Deis defines the organization, "Trackers Earth exists to re-create a village of people connected through family and the land. We lead the way in education and collaborative organization. Our method is to revive outdoor lore and traditional skills, working to restore the common sense that is no longer common." Deis also says, "Our vision is to help foster a keen appreciation for the natural world and community."

Last year, more than 2,000 people applied to work for Trackers Earth. Interviews were granted to 500 of these applicants. Of those, only eighteen were hired. Clearly, competition for a position with this organization is fierce. "Working with Trackers Earth can either be the most satisfying or the most infuriating experience of your career," says Deis. "We don't run things in the conventional way. We have highly flexible and agile development schedules in order to work with very high standards. Trackers acts more like a family than a conventional business. We're often informal, sarcastic, geeky, and definitely intense." In addition to field experience and outdoor know-how, Deis hires people who demonstrate child and group management skills.

If working for an organization like Trackers Earth sounds like the perfect job, how can you start preparing for it? Many of these types of organizations require at least a year or more of experience in outdoor camps, so start by volunteering at local camps and check to see if they offer any local educator training programs.

GLOSSARY

ACCOMMODATIONS Lodging, food, and travel-related services.

APPLICATION A request or petition, as for a job; a form used to make such a request.

APPRENTICE One who is learning—by practical experience and under skilled workers—a trade, art, or calling.

CERTIFICATION The process of being recognized as having met special qualifications (by a governmental agency or professional board) within a field.

DEDUCTION An act of taking away; something that is or may be subtracted.

DEPENDENT Someone who relies on another for support; not independent.

DISCIPLINE Orderly or prescribed conduct or pattern of behavior; self-control; a rule or system of rules governing conduct or activity.

ENTREPRENEUR One who organizes, manages, and assumes the risks of a business or enterprise.

ETHICS The discipline dealing with what is good and bad and with moral duty and obligation; a set of moral principles; a theory or system of moral values; the principles of conduct governing an individual or a group; a guiding philosophy.

EXTRACURRICULAR Not falling within the scope of a regular curriculum; of or relating to officially or semiofficially approved and usually organized student activities connected with school and usually carrying no academic credit.

HAZARDOUS Involving or exposing one to risk or harm.

INTERNSHIP A program in which an advanced student or graduate usually in a professional field gains supervised practical experience.

MOTIVATION A stimulus to or influence of action; incentive; drive.

NETWORKING The exchange of information or services among individuals, groups, or institutions; the cultivation of productive relationships for employment or business.

OPPORTUNITY A good chance for advancement or progress.

PAYCHECK Wages, salary; a check in payment of wages or salary.

RESPONSIBILITY Moral, legal, or mental accountability; reliability; trustworthiness.

RÉSUMÉ A short account of one's career and qualifications prepared typically by an applicant for a position; a set of accomplishments.

SEASONAL Affected or caused by seasonal need or availability.

STIPEND A fixed sum of money paid periodically for services or to defray expenses.

VENTURE An undertaking involving chance, risk, or danger; a speculative business enterprise.

VOLUNTEER A person who undertakes or expresses a willingness to undertake a service of his or her own free will and choice; to offer oneself as a volunteer.

Association for Experiential Education (AEE)

3775 Iris Avenue, Suite #4
Boulder, CO 80301-2043
(303) 440-8844
Web site: http://www.aee.org
AEE is a nonprofit, professional membership association dedicated to
experiential education and the students, educators, and practitioners
who utilize its philosophy.

Bureau of International Labor Affairs (ILAB)

U.S. Department of Labor
200 Constitution Avenue NW, Room C-4325
Washington, DC 20210
(202) 693-4770
Web site: http://www.dol.gov/ILAB
ILAB leads the U.S. Department of Labor's efforts to ensure that workers around the world are treated fairly and are able to share in the
benefits of the global economy. ILAB's mission is to use all available
international channels to improve working conditions, raise liv-
ing standards, protect workers' ability to exercise their rights, and
address the workplace exploitation of children and other vulnerable
populations.

Canadian International Development Agency

International Youth Internship Program
200 Promenade du Portage
Gatineau, QC K1A 0G4
Canada
(800) 230-6349
Web site: http://www.acdi-cida.gc.ca/iyip
The International Youth Internship Program (IYIP) is part of the Career
Focus stream of the government of Canada's Youth Employment

Strategy (YES). Canada's YES provides Canadian youth with tools and experience they need to launch successful careers. The objectives of the International Youth Internship Program are to provide eligible youth with international experience, skills, and knowledge that will prepare them for future employment and to provide opportunities for Canadians to increase their awareness, deepen their understanding, and engage in international development.

National Outdoor Leadership School (NOLS)
284 Lincoln Street
Lander, WY 82520-2848
(800) 710-NOLS (6657)
Web site: http://www.nols.edu
NOLS has become the leader in wilderness education. Founded in 1965 by legendary mountaineer Paul Petzoldt, NOLS takes students of all ages on remote wilderness expeditions and teaches them technical outdoor skills, leadership, and environmental ethics.

National Recreation and Park Association (NRPA)
22377 Belmont Ridge Road
Ashburn, VA 20148-4501
(800) 626-NRPA (6772)
Web site: http://www.nrpa.org/careers
NRPA's mission is to advance parks, recreation, and environmental conservation efforts that enhance the quality of life for all people. NRPA's Career Center is *the* online resource for park and recreation professionals you won't find anywhere else.

Occupational Safety & Health Administration (OSHA)
200 Constitution Avenue NW
Washington, DC 20210
(800) 321-OSHA (6742)

Web site: http://www.osha.gov/youngworkers/index.html
OSHA assures safe and healthful working conditions for working men
and women by setting and enforcing standards and by providing
training, outreach, education, and assistance.

Office of Child Labor, Forced Labor, and Human Trafficking (OCFT)

U.S. Department of Labor
200 Constitution Avenue NW, Room S-5307
Washington, DC 20210
(202) 693-4843
Web site: http://www.dol.gov/ilab/programs/ocft
OCFT's activities include research on international child labor,
forced labor, and human trafficking; funding and overseeing
cooperative agreements and contracts to organizations engaged
in efforts to eliminate exploitive child labor around the world;
and assisting in the development and implementation of U.S.
government policy on international child labor, forced labor, and
human trafficking issues.

Outdoor Industry Association (OIA)

4909 Pearl East Circle, Suite 300
Boulder, CO 80301
(303) 444-3353
Web site: http://www.outdoorindustry.org/careercenter.html
Founded in 1989, OIA is the premier trade association for companies
in the active outdoor recreation business. The Outdoor Industry
Career Center is the premier resource for outdoor jobs and career
connections in the outdoor industry. It offers one of the most com-
prehensive career and recruiting sites, matching qualified candidates that are passionate about the outdoors with the top employers in the industry.

U.S. Department of Labor
Frances Perkins Building
200 Constitution Avenue NW
Washington, DC 20210
(866) 4-USA-DOL (1-866-487-2365)
Web site: http://www.dol.gov
The Department of Labor's mission is to foster, promote, and develop
the welfare of the wage earners, job seekers, and retirees of the
United States; improve working conditions; advance opportunities for profitable employment; and assure work-related benefits
and rights.

U.S. Equal Employment Opportunity Commission (EEOC)
131 M Street NE
Washington, DC 20507
(202) 663-4900
Web site: http://www.eeoc.gov
The EEOC is responsible for enforcing federal laws that make it illegal
to discriminate against a job applicant or an employee because
of the person's race, color, religion, sex (including pregnancy),
national origin, age (forty or older), disability, or genetic information. It is also illegal to discriminate against a person because
the person complained about discrimination, filed a charge of
discrimination, or participated in an employment discrimination
investigation or lawsuit. The laws apply to all types of work situations, including hiring, firing, promotions, harassment, training,
wages, and benefits.

Youth Canada
Attn: Youth Operations Directorate
140 Promenade du Portage, Phase IV, 4D392

Mail Drop 403
Gatineau, QC K1A 0J9
Canada
(800) 935-5555
Web site: http://www.youth.gc.ca
Youth Canada is a part of Service Canada and assists young Canadians
in all aspects of their life, including job searches and career planning
and building.

WEB SITES

Due to the changing nature of Internet links, Rosen Publishing has
developed an online list of Web sites related to the subject of this
book. This site is updated regularly. Please use this link to access
the list:

http://www.rosenlinks.com/MMN/Out

FOR FURTHER READING

Bennington, Emily, and Skip Lineberg. *Effective Immediately: How to Fit In, Stand Out, and Move Up at Your First Real Job*. New York, NY: Ten Speed Press, 2010.

Berger, Lauren. *All Work, No Pay: Finding an Internship, Building Your Resume, Making Connections, and Gaining Job Experience*. Berkeley, CA: Ten Speed Press, 2012.

Berger, Sandra. *Ultimate Guide to Summer Opportunities for Teens: 200 Programs That Prepare You for College Success*. Waco, TX: Prufrock Press, 2007.

Burns, Daniel. *The First 60 Seconds: Win the Job Interview Before It Begins*. Naperville, IL: Sourcebooks, Inc., 2009.

Ferguson Publishing Company. *Discovering Careers for Your Future: Environment*. New York, NY: Ferguson, 2008.

Fryer, Julie. *The Teen's Ultimate Guide to Making Money When You Can't Get a Job: 199 Ideas for Earning Cash on Your Own Terms*. Ocala, FL: Atlantic Publishing Group Inc., 2012.

Haegele, Katie. *Cool Careers Without College for Nature Lovers*. New York, NY: Rosen Publishing, 2009.

Kirk, Amanda. *Outdoor Careers* (Field Guides to Finding a New Career). New York, NY: Ferguson, 2009.

Lehman, Jeff. *First Job—First Paycheck: How to Get the Most Out of Both Without Help from Your Parents*. Seattle, WA: Mentor Press, LLC, 2011.

Lyden, Mark. *College Students: Do This! Get Hired!: From Freshman to Ph.D.: The Secrets, Tips, Techniques, and Tricks You Need to*

Get the Full-Time Job, Co-op, or Summer Internship Position You Want. Charleston, SC: BookSurge Publishing, 2009.

Miller, Louise. *Careers for Nature Lovers and Other Outdoor Types*. New York, NY: McGraw-Hill, 2007.

Misner, Ivan, et al. *Networking Like a Pro: Turning Contacts into Connections*. Irvine, CA: Entrepreneur Press, 2010.

Payment, Simone. *Cool Careers Without College for People Who Love to Travel*. New York, NY: Rosen Publishing, 2004.

Reeves, Diane Lindsey, and Lindsey Clasen. *Career Ideas for Kids Who Like Adventure and Travel*. New York, NY: Checkmark Books, 2007.

Reeves, Diane Lindsey, and Lindsey Clasen. *Career Ideas for Kids Who Like Animals and Nature*. New York, NY: Checkmark Books, 2007.

Reeves, Ellen Gordon. *Can I Wear My Nose Ring to the Interview? A Crash Course in Finding, Landing, and Keeping Your First Real Job*. New York, NY: Workman Publishing Company, 2009.

Woodard, Eric. *Your Last Day of School: 56 Ways You Can Be a Great Intern and Turn Your Internship Into a Job*. Seattle, WA: CreateSpace, 2011.

Zack, Devora. *Networking for People Who Hate Networking: A Field Guide for Introverts, the Overwhelmed, and the Underconnected*. San Francisco, CA: Berrett-Koehler, 2010.

Zajac, Camilla. *Working Outdoors* (Real Life Guides). Grantham, England: Trotman, 2008.

BIBLIOGRAPHY

Bell, Kay. "Teen Jobs and Tax Issues: What You Need to Know."
    Fox Business, June 2, 2010. Retrieved July 2012 (http://www
    .foxbusiness.com/personal-finance/2010/06/02/teen-jobs-tax
    -issues).

Boles, Blake. *Better Than College: How to Build a Successful Life
    Without a Four-Year Degree*. Springfield, OR: Tells Peak Press,
    2012.

Boles, Blake. "How to Build a Successful Life Without a Four-Year
    Degree." The Huffington Post College Blog, July 2, 2012.
    Retrieved July 2012 (http://www.huffingtonpost.com/blake-
    boles/how-to-build-a-successful-life_b_1644107.html).

Bureau of Labor Statistics. "Occupational Outlook Handbook."
    March 29, 2012. Retrieved July 2012 (http://www.bls.gov/ooh/
    personal-care-and-service/recreation-workers.htm).

Davis, Eve. Interview with author. August 9, 2012.

Deis, Tony. Interview with author. August 8, 2012.

Devantier, Alecia T. *Extraordinary Jobs in Agriculture and Nature*.
    New York, NY: Ferguson, 2006.

Edwards, Dimitri. Interview with author. August 8, 2012.

Finley, Ellen. Interview with author. August 5, 2012.

Hershman, Livia. Interview with author. August 6, 2012.

Karas, Elizabeth. Interview with author. August 9, 2012.

Keeler, Doris. "Benefits of Volunteering for Teens." Youth Devel-
    opment at Suite 101, February 23, 2009. Retrieved July 2012

(http://suite101.com/article/benefits-of-volunteering-for
-teens-a98091).

Kekacs, Madison. Interview with author. July 28, 2012.

Lyen, Kaylee. Interview with author. August 5, 2012.

Matteson, Coogan. Interview with author. August 4, 2012.

Misner, Ivan, and Michelle R. Donovan. *The 29% Solution: 52 Weekly Networking Success Strategies*. Austin, TX: Greenleaf Book Group Press, 2008.

Orr, Caspian. Interview with author. August 4, 2012.

Orr, Nicole. Interview with author. July 29, 2012.

Palmer, Bruce. Interview with author. August 7, 2012

Sabitano, Colleen. "The Changing Role of the Intern." Internships.com. Retrieved July 2012 (http://www.internships.com/student/resources/basics/the-changing-role-of-the-intern).

Shepherd, Liam. Interview with author. August 6, 2012.

Tanabe, Gen, and Kelly Tenabe. Interview with author. August 10, 2012.

Thomason, Katie. "First Summer Jobs: Putting Your Teen to Work." eHow. Retrieved July 2012 (http://www.ehow.co.uk/feature_8276856_first-jobs-putting-teen-work.html).

Vacation Works. *Summer Jobs Worldwide 2012*. Richmond, England: Crimson Publishing, 2011.

Von Borg, Jacob. Interview with author. August 3, 2012.

INDEX

ABOUT THE AUTHOR

Tamra Orr is the author of numerous books for teen readers on careers, professional development, volunteer opportunities, and academic skill-building. She is a graduate of Ball State University and lives in the beautiful Pacific Northwest, home to some of the most amazing and inviting scenery in the world, from waterfalls to ocean beaches, big cities to high deserts. Orr enjoys reading, writing letters, and camping in the great outdoors. She is also the mother of four, two of whom are adventurous outdoor children and profiled in this book.

PHOTO CREDITS

Cover Sergey Kamshylin/Shutterstock.com; pp. 4–5 Food Carts Portland; pp. 10–11 Glow Images, Inc./Getty Images; pp. 12–13 Dave Reede/All Canada Photos/Getty Images; p. 14 Jupiterimages /Brand X Pictures/Thinkstock; p. 18 National Outdoor Leadership School (NOLS); p. 21 Greg Ceo/Taxi/Getty Images; p. 23 © iStockphoto.com/ranplett; p. 25 Comstock/Thinkstock; pp. 28–29 Noel Hendrickson/Lifesize/Getty Images; pp. 30–31 © CoolWorks .com; p. 35 Peter Muller/Cultura/Getty Images; pp. 36–37, 53 altrendo images/Stockbyte/Getty Images; p. 39 © Prisma/SuperStock; pp. 42–43 iStockphoto/Thinkstock; pp. 44–45 © iStockphoto.com /Kristian Sekulic; pp. 48–49 Jim West Image Broker/Newscom; p. 51 © AP Images; pp. 58–59 Ted Aljibe/AFP/Getty Images; pp. 60–61 National Park Service; p. 62 College of the Atlantic; p. 64 Trackers Earth; pp. 3–5, 66–80 (background image), page borders, boxed text backgrounds © iStockphoto.com/Tomasz Sowinski; back cover and remaining interior background image © iStockphoto.com/Pavel Khorenyan.

Designer: Brian Garvey; Photo Researcher: Marty Levick